LET'S
see

The Lincoln Memorial

by Marc Tyler Nobleman

Content Adviser: Linda B. Lyons, Independent Historian and Education Chair,
Art Deco Society of Washington, D.C.

Reading Adviser: Dr. Linda D. Labbo, Department of Reading Education,
College of Education, The University of Georgia

Let's See Library
Compass Point Books
Minneapolis, Minnesota

Compass Point Books
3109 West 50th Street, #115
Minneapolis, MN 55410

Visit Compass Point Books on the Internet at *www.compasspointbooks.com* or e-mail your
request to *custserv@compasspointbooks.com*

On the cover: The statue of Abraham Lincoln in the Lincoln Memorial

Photographs ©: Photo Disc, cover; White House Collection, courtesy White House Historical Association, 4;
Photo Network/Jeff Greenberg, 6; Library of Congress, 8, 10, 12; Photo Network/Mark Newman, 14;
N. Carter/North Wind Picture Archives, 16; Photo Network/Grace Davies, 18; Getty Images, 20.

Editor: Catherine Neitge
Photo Researcher: Marcie C. Spence
Designers/Page Production: Melissa Kes and Jaime Martens/Les Tranby

Library of Congress Cataloging-in-Publication Data
Nobleman, Marc Tyler.
    The Lincoln Memorial / by Marc Tyler Nobleman.
        p. cm. — (Let's see)
Summary: Discusses why, where, and how the famous monument to President Abraham Lincoln was built,
as well as what this memorial means to our country.
Includes bibliographical references and index.
ISBN 0-7565-0618-2
1. Lincoln Memorial (Washington, D.C.)—Juvenile literature. 2. Lincoln, Abraham, 1809-1865—
Monuments—Washington (D.C.)—Juvenile literature. 3. Washington (D.C.)—Buildings, structures, etc.—
Juvenile literature. [1. Lincoln Memorial (Washington, D.C.) 2. National monuments.] I. Title. II. Series.
    F203.4.L73N63 2004
    973.7'092—dc21   2003014457

Table of Contents

NOTE: In this book, words that are defined in the glossary
are in **bold** the first time they appear in the text.

4

What Is the Lincoln Memorial?

The Lincoln Memorial is a structure built to honor Abraham Lincoln. He was the 16th president of the United States. His first term of office began in 1861. In 1864, Lincoln was reelected to a second four-year term as president, but he was shot and killed in 1865.

People admired and respected Abraham Lincoln for many reasons. He believed in equality. He issued the **Emancipation Proclamation,** which freed a large number of slaves. He was very brave. He led the country through the Civil War (1861–1865). This war saved the United States. After Lincoln died, Americans wanted to remember their beloved president. They decided to build a memorial to him.

◄ Abraham Lincoln served as president from 1861 until his death in 1865.

Where Is the Lincoln Memorial?

The Lincoln Memorial is located on the National Mall in Washington, D.C. The Mall is a park that is 2 miles (3 kilometers) long. It connects the U.S. Capitol, which is the building where the U.S. Congress meets, with the Lincoln Memorial and the Washington Monument. A shorter part of the Mall connects the White House with the Jefferson Memorial. The Mall includes large areas of grass, fountains, pools, museums, and other memorials. It represents the heart of the capital city.

◀ *The Lincoln Memorial is at one end of the National Mall.*

Who Made the Lincoln Memorial?

A team of people planned and built the Lincoln Memorial. President William Howard Taft and Congress approved a bill to construct the Lincoln Memorial. Architect Henry Bacon designed it. He based his design on ancient Greek temples including the Parthenon.

Sculptor Daniel Chester French designed a large statue of Abraham Lincoln for the center of the memorial. Under French's guidance, the Piccirilli brothers carved the marble statue. Ernest C. Bairstow carved two of Lincoln's speeches into the walls. Artist Jules Guerin painted two large **murals** for the memorial. They were placed above the speeches.

◄ *A sculptor works on the Abraham Lincoln statue in about 1917.*

When Was the Lincoln Memorial Built?

People began to discuss a memorial for Abraham Lincoln soon after his death in 1865. They had to decide what kind of memorial to build and where to build it. They also needed to raise money to pay for the construction. It took many years to do these things.

Construction began on February 12, 1914. It was the 105th anniversary of Lincoln's birth. Work on the Lincoln Memorial continued during World War I (1914–1918). It took four years to carve the statue of Lincoln. It took eight years to complete the entire Lincoln Memorial. The memorial cost $3 million to build.

◄ *The Lincoln Memorial under construction in 1916*

When Did the Lincoln Memorial Open?

The **dedication** ceremony for the Lincoln Memorial was on May 30, 1922, which was Memorial Day. Dr. Robert Moton of the Tuskegee Institute delivered the **keynote address.** Tuskegee was a school for African-Americans in Alabama. Moton spoke about Lincoln's efforts to end **discrimination.** President Warren G. Harding and former President William Howard Taft also spoke.

About 50,000 people attended the ceremony. One of them was Robert Todd Lincoln. He was Abraham Lincoln's only surviving son. He was 78 years old.

◄ *Dr. Robert Moton spoke to a segregated audience during dedication ceremonies in 1922. Blacks were not allowed to sit with whites.*

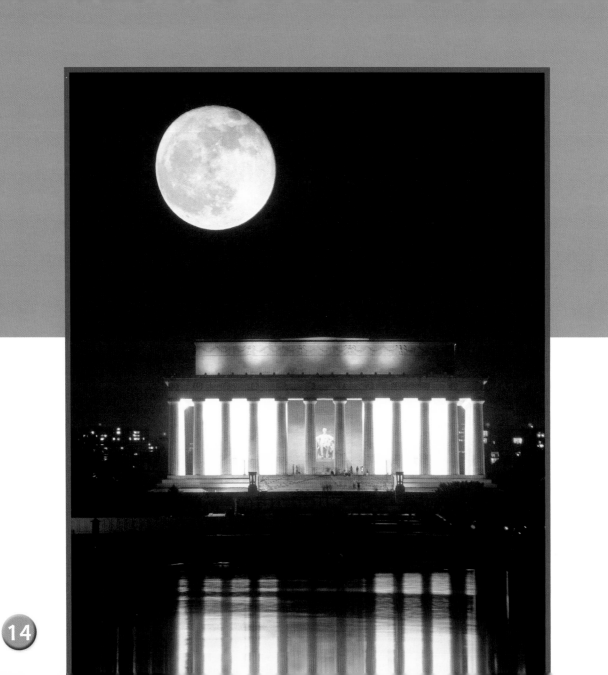

What Are the Parts of the Lincoln Memorial?

The Lincoln Memorial looks like an ancient Greek temple. The white structure is made from marble, granite, and limestone. Thirty-six **columns** run along the outside in a series called a colonnade. A large staircase, with two carved **urns** on either side, leads to the entrance.

The inside is divided into three chambers. The central chamber contains a large statue of Abraham Lincoln sitting in a chair. The words of the **Gettysburg Address** are carved into the wall of the south chamber. The words of Lincoln's second **inaugural** address are carved into the wall of the north chamber.

◀ *The statue of Lincoln faces a long, shallow reflecting pool in front of the memorial.*

IN THIS TEMPLE
AS IN THE HEARTS OF THE PEOPLE
FOR WHOM HE SAVED THE UNION
THE MEMORY OF ABRAHAM LINCOLN
IS ENSHRINED FOREVER

16

How Big Is the Lincoln Memorial?

The Lincoln Memorial is a rectangular building. It is 188 feet (57 meters) long, 118 feet (36 m) wide, and 99 feet (30 m) high.

The columns surrounding the Lincoln Memorial are 44 feet (13 m) high. They are spread out a little bit at the entrance to make it look more important.

The statue of Abraham Lincoln is 19 feet (6 m) high. If the statue could stand, it would be 28 feet (9 m) high. It weighs 175 tons (159 metric tons).

◄ *Although Abraham Lincoln is resting in his chair, he appears strong and thoughtful.*

How Can You See the Lincoln Memorial?

More than a million people visit the Lincoln Memorial every year. When you visit it, you can also walk to other memorials and monuments on the National Mall.

The Lincoln Memorial is lit up at night. Park rangers are on duty from 8 a.m. to midnight daily, except Christmas. The rangers give tours and can tell you more about Abraham Lincoln and the Lincoln Memorial. Admission is free.

◄ *The Lincoln Memorial is always open for visitors.*

What Does the Lincoln Memorial Mean to People?

The Lincoln Memorial is a tribute to President Abraham Lincoln. To some, it also serves as a Civil War memorial and a symbol of the **civil rights movement.**

Abraham Lincoln believed in equality and freedom for all. He believed that people should not be enslaved. He believed that people should live in peace with one another.

The Lincoln Memorial remains a monument to these ideas.

◄ *In 1963, Dr. Martin Luther King Jr. gave his famous "I Have a Dream" speech to thousands of people gathered at the Lincoln Memorial.*

Glossary

civil rights movement—in the 1950s and 1960s, an effort to gain African-Americans equal treatment in the United States

column—an upright structure shaped like a post

dedication—an opening observance

discrimination—treating people unfairly because of their race, religion, sex, or age

Emancipation Proclamation—a document signed on January 1, 1863, by President Lincoln that freed slaves in the South

Gettysburg Address—a speech given on November 19, 1863, by President Lincoln; it is one of the most famous speeches in history

inaugural—relating to a president's swearing-in ceremony, which is when the term of office begins

keynote address—main speech at an event

mural—wall painting

urn—a vase set on a base

Did You Know?

• The outside of the Lincoln Memorial has 36 columns because there were 36 states in the Union when Abraham Lincoln died. The names of these states are listed just above the colonnade. Above them, on the attic of the building, are the names of the 48 states that existed when the memorial was dedicated in 1922.

• The Lincoln Memorial is made from marble and limestone from several states including Alabama, Colorado, Georgia, Indiana, and Tennessee.

• An important concert took place at the Lincoln Memorial in 1939. Famous singer Marian Anderson had planned to sing at Constitution Hall in Washington, D.C. It was owned by the Daughters of the American Revolution (DAR). They would not let her perform there because she was black. So First Lady Eleanor Roosevelt and others set up a concert for her at the Lincoln Memorial. Marian Anderson sang for more than 75,000 people.

Want to Know More?

In the Library

Binns, Tristan Boyer. *The Lincoln Memorial.*
    Crystal Lake, Ill.: Heinemann Library, 2001.
January, Brendan. *The National Mall.*
    Danbury, Conn.: Children's Press, 2000.
Kent, Deborah. *The Lincoln Memorial.*
    Danbury, Conn.: Children's Press, 1997.
Raatma, Lucia. *Abraham Lincoln.*
    Minneapolis: Compass Point Books, 2001.

On the Web

For more information on the *Lincoln Memorial,* use FactHound to track down Web sites related to this book.

1. Go to *www.compasspointbooks.com/facthound*
2. Type in this book ID: 0756506182
3. Click on the *Fetch It* button.

Your trusty FactHound will fetch the best Web sites for you!

Through the Mail

Lincoln Memorial
900 Ohio Drive S.W.
Washington, DC 20024
To write for information about the Lincoln Memorial

On the Road

Lincoln Memorial
23rd Street N.W.
Washington, DC
Metro stop: Foggy Bottom
202/426-6841
To visit the Lincoln Memorial; park rangers are on duty from 8 a.m. to midnight daily, except Christmas

Index

About the Author

Marc Tyler Nobleman has written more than 30 books for young readers. He has also written for a History Channel show called "The Great American History Quiz" and for several children's magazines including Nickelodeon, Highlights for Children, and Read (a Weekly Reader publication). He is also a cartoonist, and his single panels have appeared in more than 100 magazines internationally. He lives in Connecticut.